LAKERS LEGENDS ALPHABET

Words by Robin Feiner

A is for Kareem Abdul-Jabbar. The Captain was a giant yet graceful center who retired with an NBA-record 38,387 points. His legendary skyhook, considered the most unguardable shot in league history, helped him to 13 All-Star Games, 3 MVP awards and 5 NBA titles in his 14 Laker seasons!

B is for **B**ob McAdoo. Unlike most big men, McAdoo had a sweet shooting touch. An MVP and three-time scoring leader in the 1970s, he sacrificed playing time for success when he joined the team in 1981. A favorite of coach Pat Riley, McAdoo's bench scoring helped the Lakers win the 1982 and 1985 titles.

C is for Wilt **C**hamberlain. This 7'1" center dominated so much that the NBA had to change the rules to level the playing field! The Big Dipper played for the Lakers from 1968–73, making the All-Star Game and leading the league in rebounding four times. His 23,924 career rebounds is still a record today.

D is for Vlade **D**ivac.
This lovable Serb paved the way for Europeans to play in the NBA when the Lakers drafted him in 1989. On the court, he dazzled with his smart passing and smooth footwork. Off the court, his smile and charm made him a fan favorite despite speaking little English.

E is for **El**gin Baylor.
In his legendary 14-year Hall of Fame career, The Man with a Thousand Moves changed the way the game was played. Taking the game to new heights, the athletic 11-time All-Star stunned crowds with his twists and turns on the court, and by acrobatically hanging in the air!

F is for Derek **F**isher. Though often outshone by other stars, the Lakers probably wouldn't have won five of their titles without this dependable point guard and favorite teammate of Kobe Bryant. Fish's 2004 Western Conference Semifinals buzzer beater remains a legendary L.A. hoops moment.

G is for George Mikan. Considered the NBA's first superstar, Mr. Basketball played his seven-year career with the Minneapolis Lakers. Mikan's legendary rebounding, shot-blocking and hook shot proved that big men could tower over the game. The 24-second shot clock was created after players wasted time holding the ball so he couldn't get it!

Hh

H is for Chick **H**earn. The voice of the Lakers for 42 years, Hearn announced a record 3,338 straight regular-season games from 1965–2001. Calling from his "word's-eye view," he invented Chickisms like "slam dunk" and "air ball," which have become part of the legendary game.

I is for Darrall **I**mhoff. Suiting up with fellow legends Jerry West and Elgin Baylor, this rugged player spent four seasons with the Lakers from 1964–68. Nicknamed The Ax, he also made one All-Star team and helped the Lakers reach the NBA Finals three times.

Jj

J is for Jerry West. Mr. Clutch was a scoring machine and tough-nosed defender. An All-Star in each of his 14 legendary seasons, West retired with a franchise-record 25,192 career points, and is the man behind the silhouette featured on the NBA logo. Legendary!

K is for **K**obe Bryant. Black Mamba's legendary toughness and leadership helped his team win five NBA titles. Playing his entire 20-season career with the Lakers, he retired in 2016 with franchise records in points (33,643) and games played (1,346), and a mountain of iconic moments. A true legend who will never be forgotten.

L is for **L**eBron James.
There's never been a player
with the size, strength, speed
and skill of King James.
He joined the Lakers in 2018
and reached legendary status
the following season with an
iconic MVP performance in
the Finals that earned the
team its 17th championship.

M is for **M**agic Johnson. One of the greatest Lakers of all time, this 6'9" legend's height, strength, speed and silky skills redefined the point guard position. He led the 1980s 'Showtime' Lakers to five NBA titles, and won three MVP awards during his Hall of Fame career. His play was simply magic.

N is for Norm Nixon. Playing his first six NBA seasons with the Lakers, Nixon was the team's point guard before all-time great Magic Johnson took over. Winning titles with a team full of Hall of Famers in 1980 and 1982, the often-underrated Nixon led in scoring during that second playoff run.

O is for Shaquille **O**'Neal. The only thing bigger than his frame was his legendary personality. Quotable off the court, and destructive on it, this game-changing center bulldozed opponents near the rim. His dominance saw him named NBA Finals MVP for each of the Lakers' titles during their historic 2000–02 three-peat.

P is for **P**au Gasol.
This Spanish center teamed up with Kobe Bryant to win back-to-back titles in 2009 and 2010. A skilled big man who made plays for his teammates while also scoring, rebounding and protecting the rim, Gasol made three All-Star teams in his six full Lakers seasons.

Q is for Nick the **Q**uick. Speedy point guard Nick Van Exel was known for his flashy play during his five years with the Lakers from 1993–98. Even though the team wasn't a serious title contender, Nick wowed fans with his legendary dribbling, pinpoint passing and exciting buzzer beaters.

R is for Pat Riley.
Riley's 1980s Lakers teams were fast-paced and exciting. Known for his toughness, the coach led the 'Showtime' squad to four titles. While the team had a powerful offense, Riley's defensive structure forced opponents to make mistakes. He also won a title playing for the 1971–72 Lakers.

S is for Byron Scott. Scott's amazing athleticism and defensive toughness were key to the 1980s Lakers reaching their 'Showtime' potential. But he could score, too, leading the 1987–88 title-winning team during the regular season. Returning for one final season in 1996, Scott helped mentor a young Kobe Bryant.

T is for Mychal **T**hompson. Playing backup center to Hall-of-Famer Kareem Abdul-Jabbar, Thompson was part of two championship teams for the Lakers in 1987 and 1988. Continuing to contribute to the game off the court, he has entertained Lakers fans with years of humorous radio commentary.

U is for Uncle P.
Years before becoming the Lakers' general manager in 2017, Rob Pelinka was Kobe Bryant's agent and godfather to his daughter Gianna, who nicknamed him Uncle P. He was the man who helped bring LeBron James and Anthony Davis to the Lakers and return the team to title-winning glory.

V is for **V**ern Mikkelsen. Back in the 1950s, this bruising forward was a rugged and dependable defender and scorer for four-time champions, the Minneapolis Lakers. Mikkelsen missed only five games in 10 seasons, retiring as the sixth NBA player to score 10,000 points, and with a record 127 games fouled out.

W is for James Worthy.
Big Game James played
his 12-year career with the
Lakers, winning three titles
with the 1980s 'Showtime'
team. The seven-time All-Star
is certainly worthy of his
legendary status, with turn-
around baseline jumpers in
the post that were just as
deadly as his Statue of
Liberty dunks.

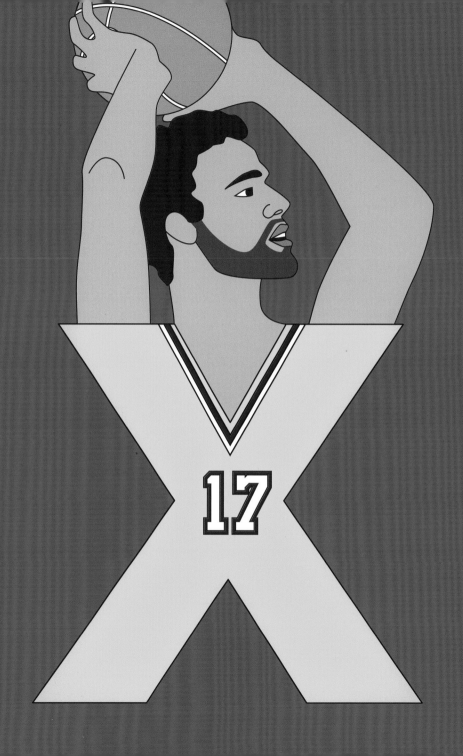

X is for Rick Fox.
Fox did a lot of the little things that helped the Lakers three-peat from 1999–2002, sacrificing his own stats to make the right play so stars like Shaquille O'Neal and Kobe Bryant could shine brighter. Fox was also an actor, which made him a great fit for L.A.

Y is for Nick **Y**oung. Probably known more for his on- and off-court antics than his skill, Swaggy P's main role was to shoot threes during his four Lakers seasons. He set a franchise record with 36 threes over an 8-game stretch in the 2016–17 season.

Z is for the Zen Master, Phil Jackson. He introduced mindfulness methods in his coaching and changed the game forever. Winning five titles in his 11 Lakers seasons, including a three-peat with Shaq and Kobe in his first three seasons from 1999–2002, Jackson is one of the greatest coaches in sports history.

The ever-expanding legendary library

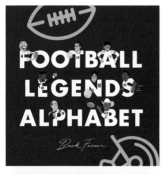

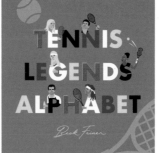

EXPLORE THESE LEGENDARY ALPHABETS & MORE AT WWW.ALPHABETLEGENDS.COM

LAKERS LEGENDS ALPHABET
www.alphabetlegends.com

Published by Alphabet Legends Pty Ltd in 2021
Created by Beck Feiner
Copyright © Alphabet Legends Pty Ltd 2021

Printed and bound in China.

9780648962861

ALPHABET LEGENDS